Book Index

Pages	Title	Author	Genre

Book Index

Title	Author	Genre	Pages

Book Index

Pages	Title	Author	Genre

Book Index

Title	Author	Genre	Pages

Book Wishlist

✓	Title	Author	Genre
☐			
☐			
☐			
☐			
☐			
☐			
☐			
☐			
☐			
☐			
☐			
☐			
☐			
☐			
☐			
☐			
☐			
☐			
☐			
☐			
☐			
☐			
☐			

Book Wishlist

Title	Author	Genre	✓
			☐
			☐
			☐
			☐
			☐
			☐
			☐
			☐
			☐
			☐
			☐
			☐
			☐
			☐
			☐
			☐
			☐
			☐
			☐
			☐
			☐
			☐
			☐
			☐
			☐
			☐
			☐

Book Wishlist

✔	Title	Author	Genre
☐			
☐			
☐			
☐			
☐			
☐			
☐			
☐			
☐			
☐			
☐			
☐			
☐			
☐			
☐			
☐			
☐			
☐			
☐			
☐			
☐			
☐			
☐			
☐			
☐			

Book Review

Title:

Author:

Date Started: **Date Finished:**

Rating: ☆ ☆ ☆ ☆ ☆

Review:

Quotes:

One Book One Reason:

No.	# Book Review

Title:

Author:

Date Started: **Date Finished:**

Rating: ☆ ☆ ☆ ☆ ☆

Review:

Quotes:

One Book One Reason:

Book Review

Title:

Author:

Date Started: **Date Finished:**

Rating: ☆ ☆ ☆ ☆ ☆

Review:

Quotes:

One Book One Reason:

No.	**Book Review**

Title:

Author:

Date Started: **Date Finished:**

Rating: ☆ ☆ ☆ ☆ ☆

Review:

Quotes:

One Book One Reason:

Book Review

Title:

Author:

Date Started: **Date Finished:**

Rating: ☆☆☆☆☆

Review:

Quotes:

One Book One Reason:

No.	# Book Review

Title:

Author:

Date Started: **Date Finished:**

Rating: ☆ ☆ ☆ ☆ ☆

Review:

Quotes:

One Book One Reason:

Book Review

Title:

Author:

Date Started: **Date Finished:**

Rating: ☆ ☆ ☆ ☆ ☆

Review:

Quotes:

One Book One Reason:

No.	# Book Review

Title:

Author:

Date Started: **Date Finished:**

Rating: ☆☆☆☆☆

Review:

Quotes:

One Book One Reason:

Book Review

No.

Title:

Author:

Date Started: **Date Finished:**

Rating: ☆ ☆ ☆ ☆ ☆

Review:

Quotes:

One Book One Reason:

No.	# Book Review

Title:

Author:

Date Started: **Date Finished:**

Rating: ☆ ☆ ☆ ☆ ☆

Review:

Quotes:

One Book One Reason:

Book Review

Title:

Author:

Date Started: **Date Finished:**

Rating: ☆ ☆ ☆ ☆ ☆

Review:

Quotes:

One Book One Reason:

No.	# Book Review

Title:

Author:

Date Started: **Date Finished:**

Rating: ☆ ☆ ☆ ☆ ☆

Review:

Quotes:

One Book One Reason:

Book Review

No.

Title:

Author:

Date Started: **Date Finished:**

Rating: ☆ ☆ ☆ ☆ ☆

Review:

Quotes:

One Book One Reason:

No.	# Book Review

Title:

Author:

Date Started: **Date Finished:**

Rating: ☆ ☆ ☆ ☆ ☆

Review:

Quotes:

One Book One Reason:

Book Review

Title:

Author:

Date Started: **Date Finished:**

Rating: ☆ ☆ ☆ ☆ ☆

Review:

Quotes:

One Book One Reason:

No.	# Book Review

Title:

Author:

Date Started: **Date Finished:**

Rating: ☆ ☆ ☆ ☆ ☆

Review:

Quotes:

One Book One Reason:

Book Review

No.

Title:

Author:

Date Started: **Date Finished:**

Rating: ☆ ☆ ☆ ☆ ☆

Review:

Quotes:

One Book One Reason:

No.	# Book Review

Title:

Author:

Date Started: **Date Finished:**

Rating: ☆ ☆ ☆ ☆ ☆

Review:

Quotes:

One Book One Reason:

Book Review

Title:

Author:

Date Started: **Date Finished:**

Rating: ☆ ☆ ☆ ☆ ☆

Review:

Quotes:

One Book One Reason:

No.	# Book Review

Title:

Author:

Date Started: **Date Finished:**

Rating: ☆ ☆ ☆ ☆ ☆

Review:

Quotes:

One Book One Reason:

Book Review

No.

Title:

Author:

Date Started: **Date Finished:**

Rating: ☆ ☆ ☆ ☆ ☆

Review:

Quotes:

One Book One Reason:

No.	# Book Review

Title:

Author:

Date Started: **Date Finished:**

Rating: ☆ ☆ ☆ ☆ ☆

Review:

Quotes:

One Book One Reason:

Book Review

No.

Title:

Author:

Date Started: **Date Finished:**

Rating: ☆ ☆ ☆ ☆ ☆

Review:

Quotes:

One Book One Reason:

No.	**Book Review**

Title:

Author:

Date Started: **Date Finished:**

Rating: ☆ ☆ ☆ ☆ ☆

Review:

Quotes:

One Book One Reason:

Book Review

No.

Title:

Author:

Date Started: Date Finished:

Rating: ☆☆☆☆☆

Review:

Quotes:

One Book One Reason:

No.	# Book Review

Title:

Author:

Date Started: **Date Finished:**

Rating: ☆ ☆ ☆ ☆ ☆

Review:

Quotes:

One Book One Reason:

Book Review

No.

Title:

Author:

Date Started: **Date Finished:**

Rating: ☆ ☆ ☆ ☆ ☆

Review:

Quotes:

One Book One Reason:

No.	Book Review

Title:

Author:

Date Started: **Date Finished:**

Rating: ☆ ☆ ☆ ☆ ☆

Review:

Quotes:

One Book One Reason:

Book Review

Title:

Author:

Date Started: **Date Finished:**

Rating: ☆ ☆ ☆ ☆ ☆

Review:

Quotes:

One Book One Reason:

No.	# Book Review

Title:

Author:

Date Started: **Date Finished:**

Rating: ☆ ☆ ☆ ☆ ☆

Review:

Quotes:

One Book One Reason:

Book Review

No.

Title:

Author:

Date Started: **Date Finished:**

Rating: ☆ ☆ ☆ ☆ ☆

Review:

Quotes:

One Book One Reason:

No.	# Book Review

Title:

Author:

Date Started: **Date Finished:**

Rating: ☆ ☆ ☆ ☆ ☆

Review:

Quotes:

One Book One Reason:

Book Review

No.

Title:

Author:

Date Started: **Date Finished:**

Rating: ☆ ☆ ☆ ☆ ☆

Review:

Quotes:

One Book One Reason:

No.	Book Review

Title:

Author:

Date Started: **Date Finished:**

Rating: ☆ ☆ ☆ ☆ ☆

Review:

Quotes:

One Book One Reason:

Book Review

No.

Title:

Author:

Date Started: **Date Finished:**

Rating: ☆ ☆ ☆ ☆ ☆

Review:

Quotes:

One Book One Reason:

No.	# Book Review

Title:

Author:

Date Started: **Date Finished:**

Rating: ☆ ☆ ☆ ☆ ☆

Review:

Quotes:

One Book One Reason:

Book Review

Title:

Author:

Date Started: **Date Finished:**

Rating: ☆ ☆ ☆ ☆ ☆

Review:

Quotes:

One Book One Reason:

No.	# Book Review

Title:

Author:

Date Started: **Date Finished:**

Rating: ☆ ☆ ☆ ☆ ☆

Review:

Quotes:

One Book One Reason:

Book Review

Title:

Author:

Date Started: **Date Finished:**

Rating: ☆ ☆ ☆ ☆ ☆

Review:

Quotes:

One Book One Reason:

No.	# Book Review

Title:

Author:

Date Started: **Date Finished:**

Rating: ☆ ☆ ☆ ☆ ☆

Review:

Quotes:

One Book One Reason:

Book Review

Title:

Author:

Date Started: **Date Finished:**

Rating: ☆ ☆ ☆ ☆ ☆

Review:

Quotes:

One Book One Reason:

No.	# Book Review

Title:

Author:

Date Started: **Date Finished:**

Rating: ☆ ☆ ☆ ☆ ☆

Review:

Quotes:

One Book One Reason:

Book Review

Title:

Author:

Date Started: **Date Finished:**

Rating: ☆ ☆ ☆ ☆ ☆

Review:

Quotes:

One Book One Reason:

No.	# Book Review

Title:

Author:

Date Started: **Date Finished:**

Rating: ☆ ☆ ☆ ☆ ☆

Review:

Quotes:

One Book One Reason:

Book Review

No.

Title:

Author:

Date Started:　　　　　　　　**Date Finished:**

Rating: ☆ ☆ ☆ ☆ ☆

Review:

Quotes:

One Book One Reason:

No.	# Book Review

Title:

Author:

Date Started: **Date Finished:**

Rating: ☆ ☆ ☆ ☆ ☆

Review:

Quotes:

One Book One Reason:

Book Review

No.

Title:

Author:

Date Started: **Date Finished:**

Rating: ☆ ☆ ☆ ☆ ☆

Review:

Quotes:

One Book One Reason:

No.	# Book Review

Title:

Author:

Date Started: **Date Finished:**

Rating: ☆ ☆ ☆ ☆ ☆

Review:

Quotes:

One Book One Reason:

Book Review

No.

Title:

Author:

Date Started: **Date Finished:**

Rating: ☆ ☆ ☆ ☆ ☆

Review:

Quotes:

One Book One Reason:

No.	**Book Review**

Title:

Author:

Date Started: **Date Finished:**

Rating: ☆ ☆ ☆ ☆ ☆

Review:

Quotes:

One Book One Reason:

Book Review

No.

Title:

Author:

Date Started: **Date Finished:**

Rating: ☆☆☆☆☆

Review:

Quotes:

One Book One Reason:

No.	# Book Review

Title:

Author:

Date Started: **Date Finished:**

Rating: ☆ ☆ ☆ ☆ ☆

Review:

Quotes:

One Book One Reason:

Book Review

Title:

Author:

Date Started: **Date Finished:**

Rating: ☆ ☆ ☆ ☆ ☆

Review:

Quotes:

One Book One Reason:

No.	# Book Review

Title:

Author:

Date Started: **Date Finished:**

Rating: ☆ ☆ ☆ ☆ ☆

Review:

Quotes:

One Book One Reason:

Book Review

No.

Title:

Author:

Date Started: Date Finished:

Rating: ☆ ☆ ☆ ☆ ☆

Review:

Quotes:

One Book One Reason:

No.	# Book Review

Title:

Author:

Date Started: **Date Finished:**

Rating: ☆ ☆ ☆ ☆ ☆

Review:

Quotes:

One Book One Reason:

Book Review

No.

Title:

Author:

Date Started: **Date Finished:**

Rating: ☆ ☆ ☆ ☆ ☆

Review:

Quotes:

One Book One Reason:

No.	# Book Review

Title:

Author:

Date Started: **Date Finished:**

Rating: ☆ ☆ ☆ ☆ ☆

Review:

Quotes:

One Book One Reason:

Book Review

No.

Title:

Author:

Date Started: Date Finished:

Rating: ☆ ☆ ☆ ☆ ☆

Review:

Quotes:

One Book One Reason:

No.	# Book Review

Title:

Author:

Date Started: **Date Finished:**

Rating: ☆ ☆ ☆ ☆ ☆

Review:

Quotes:

One Book One Reason:

Book Review

Title:

Author:

Date Started: **Date Finished:**

Rating: ☆ ☆ ☆ ☆ ☆

Review:

Quotes:

One Book One Reason:

No.	# Book Review

Title:

Author:

Date Started: **Date Finished:**

Rating: ☆ ☆ ☆ ☆ ☆

Review:

Quotes:

One Book One Reason:

Book Review

Title:

Author:

Date Started: **Date Finished:**

Rating: ☆ ☆ ☆ ☆ ☆

Review:

Quotes:

One Book One Reason:

No.	**Book Review**

Title:

Author:

Date Started: **Date Finished:**

Rating: ☆ ☆ ☆ ☆ ☆

Review:

Quotes:

One Book One Reason:

Book Review

No.

Title:

Author:

Date Started: **Date Finished:**

Rating: ☆ ☆ ☆ ☆ ☆

Review:

Quotes:

One Book One Reason:

No.	Book Review

Title:

Author:

Date Started: **Date Finished:**

Rating: ☆ ☆ ☆ ☆ ☆

Review:

Quotes:

One Book One Reason:

Book Review

No.

Title:

Author:

Date Started: **Date Finished:**

Rating: ☆☆☆☆☆

Review:

Quotes:

One Book One Reason:

No.	# Book Review

Title:

Author:

Date Started: **Date Finished:**

Rating: ☆ ☆ ☆ ☆ ☆

Review:

Quotes:

One Book One Reason:

Book Review

No.

Title:

Author:

Date Started: **Date Finished:**

Rating: ☆ ☆ ☆ ☆ ☆

Review:

Quotes:

One Book One Reason:

No.	# Book Review

Title:

Author:

Date Started: **Date Finished:**

Rating: ☆ ☆ ☆ ☆ ☆

Review:

Quotes:

One Book One Reason:

Book Review

No.

Title:

Author:

Date Started: **Date Finished:**

Rating: ☆ ☆ ☆ ☆ ☆

Review:

Quotes:

One Book One Reason:

No.	# Book Review

Title:

Author:

Date Started: **Date Finished:**

Rating: ☆ ☆ ☆ ☆ ☆

Review:

Quotes:

One Book One Reason:

Book Review

Title:

Author:

Date Started: **Date Finished:**

Rating: ☆ ☆ ☆ ☆ ☆

Review:

Quotes:

One Book One Reason:

No.	# Book Review

Title:

Author:

Date Started: **Date Finished:**

Rating: ☆ ☆ ☆ ☆ ☆

Review:

Quotes:

One Book One Reason:

Book Review

No.

Title:

Author:

Date Started: **Date Finished:**

Rating: ☆☆☆☆☆

Review:

Quotes:

One Book One Reason:

No.	**Book Review**

Title:

Author:

Date Started: **Date Finished:**

Rating: ☆ ☆ ☆ ☆ ☆

Review:

Quotes:

One Book One Reason:

Book Review

No.

Title:

Author:

Date Started: **Date Finished:**

Rating: ☆ ☆ ☆ ☆ ☆

Review:

Quotes:

One Book One Reason:

No.	# Book Review

Title:

Author:

Date Started: **Date Finished:**

Rating: ☆ ☆ ☆ ☆ ☆

Review:

Quotes:

One Book One Reason:

Book Review

No.

Title:

Author:

Date Started: **Date Finished:**

Rating: ☆ ☆ ☆ ☆ ☆

Review:

Quotes:

One Book One Reason:

No.	# Book Review

Title:

Author:

Date Started: **Date Finished:**

Rating: ☆ ☆ ☆ ☆ ☆

Review:

Quotes:

One Book One Reason:

Book Review

Title:

Author:

Date Started: **Date Finished:**

Rating: ☆ ☆ ☆ ☆ ☆

Review:

Quotes:

One Book One Reason:

No.	# Book Review

Title:

Author:

Date Started: **Date Finished:**

Rating: ☆ ☆ ☆ ☆ ☆

Review:

Quotes:

One Book One Reason:

Book Review

No.

Title:

Author:

Date Started: **Date Finished:**

Rating: ☆☆☆☆☆

Review:

Quotes:

One Book One Reason:

No.	# Book Review

Title:

Author:

Date Started: **Date Finished:**

Rating: ☆ ☆ ☆ ☆ ☆

Review:

Quotes:

One Book One Reason:

Book Review

No.

Title:

Author:

Date Started: **Date Finished:**

Rating: ☆ ☆ ☆ ☆ ☆

Review:

Quotes:

One Book One Reason:

No.	# Book Review

Title:

Author:

Date Started: **Date Finished:**

Rating: ☆☆☆☆☆

Review:

Quotes:

One Book One Reason:

Book Review

Title:

Author:

Date Started: **Date Finished:**

Rating: ☆ ☆ ☆ ☆ ☆

Review:

Quotes:

One Book One Reason:

No.	**Book Review**

Title:

Author:

Date Started: **Date Finished:**

Rating: ☆ ☆ ☆ ☆ ☆

Review:

Quotes:

One Book One Reason:

Book Review

No.

Title:

Author:

Date Started: **Date Finished:**

Rating: ☆ ☆ ☆ ☆ ☆

Review:

Quotes:

One Book One Reason:

No.	**Book Review**

Title:

Author:

Date Started: **Date Finished:**

Rating: ☆ ☆ ☆ ☆ ☆

Review:

Quotes:

One Book One Reason:

Book Review

Title:

Author:

Date Started: **Date Finished:**

Rating: ☆ ☆ ☆ ☆ ☆

Review:

Quotes:

One Book One Reason:

No.	# Book Review

Title:

Author:

Date Started: **Date Finished:**

Rating: ☆ ☆ ☆ ☆ ☆

Review:

Quotes:

One Book One Reason:

Book Review

No.

Title:

Author:

Date Started: **Date Finished:**

Rating: ☆ ☆ ☆ ☆ ☆

Review:

Quotes:

One Book One Reason:

No.	**Book Review**

Title:

Author:

Date Started: **Date Finished:**

Rating: ☆ ☆ ☆ ☆ ☆

Review:

Quotes:

One Book One Reason:

Book Review

No.

Title:

Author:

Date Started: Date Finished:

Rating: ☆ ☆ ☆ ☆ ☆

Review:

Quotes:

One Book One Reason:

No.	# Book Review

Title:

Author:

Date Started: **Date Finished:**

Rating: ☆ ☆ ☆ ☆ ☆

Review:

Quotes:

One Book One Reason:

Book Review

Title:

Author:

Date Started: **Date Finished:**

Rating: ☆ ☆ ☆ ☆ ☆

Review:

Quotes:

One Book One Reason:

No.	**Book Review**

Title:

Author:

Date Started: **Date Finished:**

Rating: ☆☆☆☆☆

Review:

Quotes:

One Book One Reason:

Book Review

No.

Title:

Author:

Date Started: **Date Finished:**

Rating: ☆☆☆☆☆

Review:

Quotes:

One Book One Reason:

No.	# Book Review

Title:

Author:

Date Started: **Date Finished:**

Rating: ☆ ☆ ☆ ☆ ☆

Review:

Quotes:

One Book One Reason:

Made in the USA
Columbia, SC
23 November 2018